D0369163

Is Your Dog Gay?

For Anne Hall -V.R.

SIMON & SCHUSTER
Rockefeller Center, 1230 Avenue of the Americas, New York, NY 10020

SIMON & SCHUSTER and colophon are registered trademarks
of Simon & Schuster, Inc.

For information about special discounts for bulk purchases,
please contact Simon & Schuster Special Sales at
1-800-456-6798 or business@simonandschuster.com

Designed by Charles Kreloff

Manufactured in Mexico

1 3 5 7 9 10 8 6 4 2

Library of Congress Cataloging-in-Publication Data
Kreloff, Charles.
Is your dog gay? / by Charles Kreloff and Patty Brown ;
drawings by Victoria Roberts.
     p.   cm.
1. Dogs—Humor. 2. Homosexuality—Humor. I. Brown, Patty. II. Title.
PN6231.D68 K67   2004   818'.6—dc22   2004056528

ISBN 0-7432-7077-0

Is Your Dog Gay?

by Charles Kreloff and Patty Brown

Drawings by Victoria Roberts

A Roundtable Press Book

Simon & Schuster

New York   London   Toronto   Sydney

Have you ever found
yourself pondering your dog's
sexual preference?

If so, consider the following...

Does your dog chew
only on Manolos?

Do you suspect your dog is sharing confidences with the groomer?

Does your dog accept doggie bags only from The Four Seasons, "21," or the Condé Nast cafeteria?

Does your dog pee exclusively on *Vogue*?

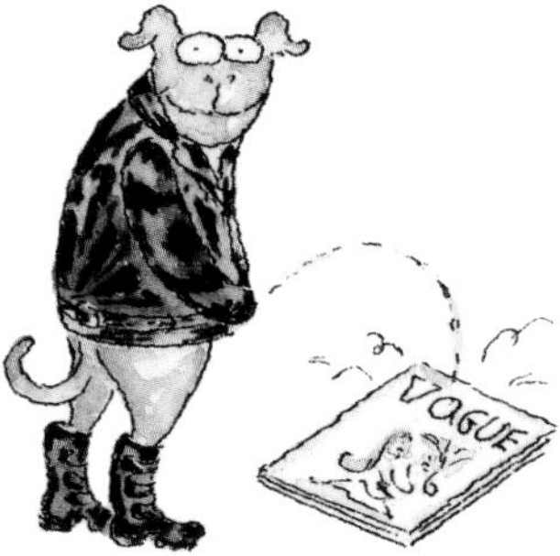
VOGUE

Does your dog insist on interviewing
the dog walker?

Does your dog assume the
top doggie position?

Must your dog's biscotti be served
with a double espresso?

Is this what doggie style
means in your house?

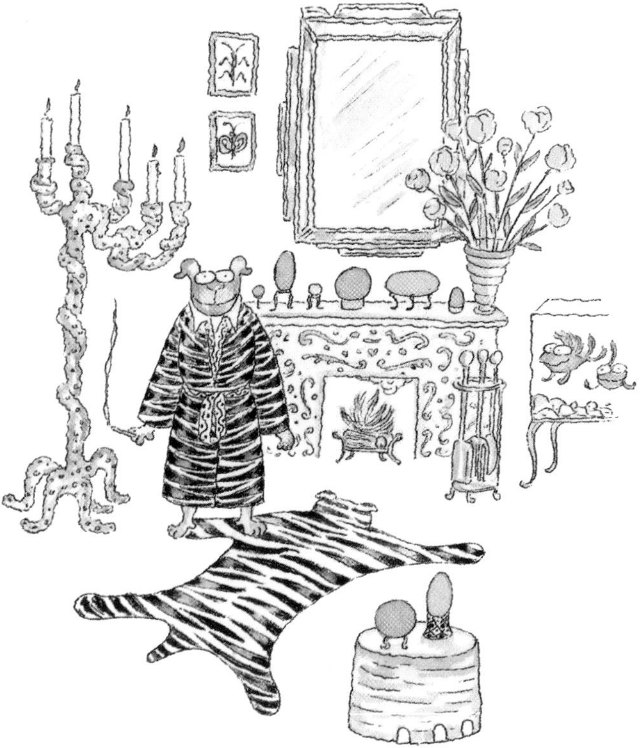

Is this why it takes so long
to head out for walkies?

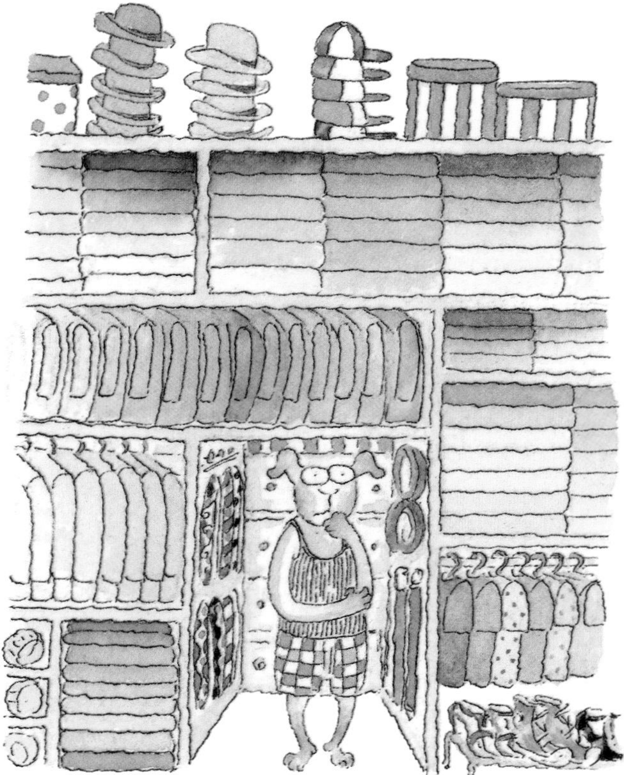

Is this your dog's idea
of regular exercise?

Has your dog turned into
a complete bitch?

Does your dog require
his own wet bar?

is the doghouse Bauhaus?

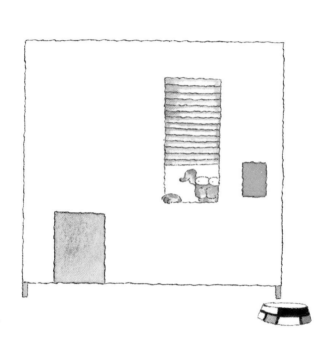

Do bones bring out
your dog's artistic side?

Does doggie swoon over
that lost Maria Callas recording
that only he can hear?

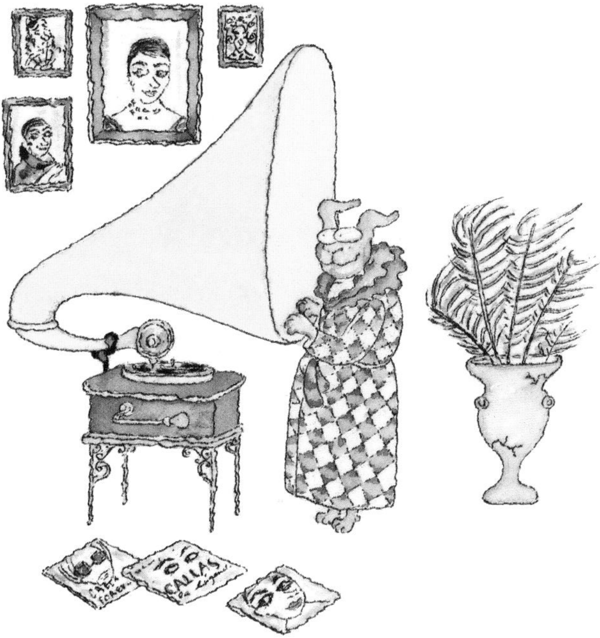
CALLAS

Does doggie bottle his own scent?

Does your dog exhibit
obsessive behavior when choosing
a bandanna?

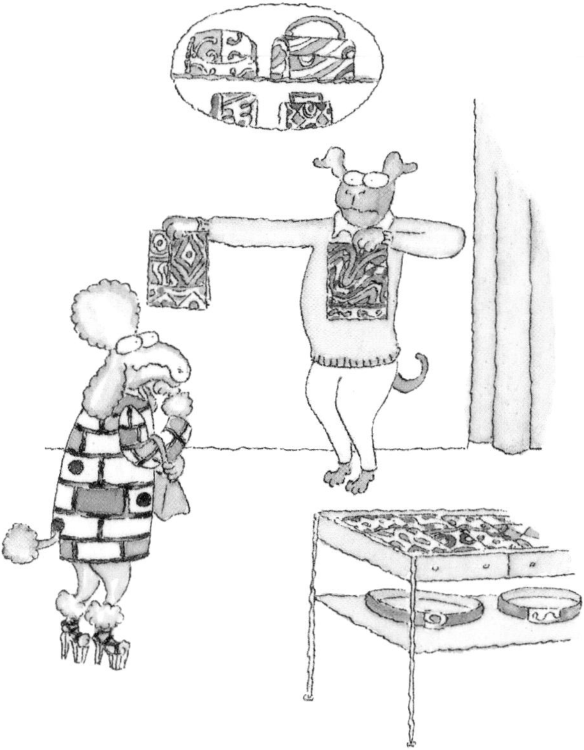

Is this your dog's idea of fetch?

Does your dog look forward to
a day at "The Baths"?

Must all of your dog's coats be
custom tailored on Savile Row?

Is this one of your dog's favorite tricks?

Does your dog love nothing better
than a fabulous show?

BEST
IN
⭐ SHOW

Have you found evidence of
a snide memoir lying about?

Is your copy of *Blue Dog*
suspiciously dog-eared?

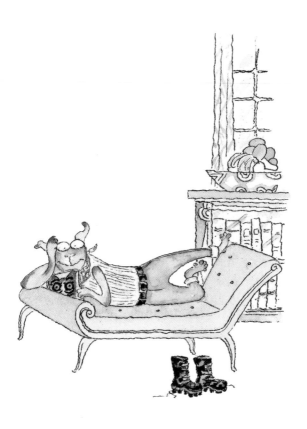

Are his dog toys only for display?

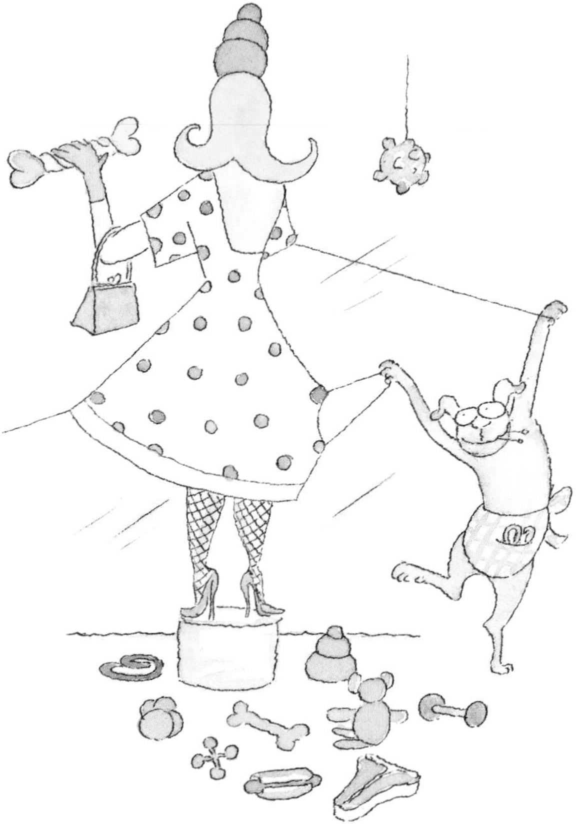

Does doggie *really* love leather?

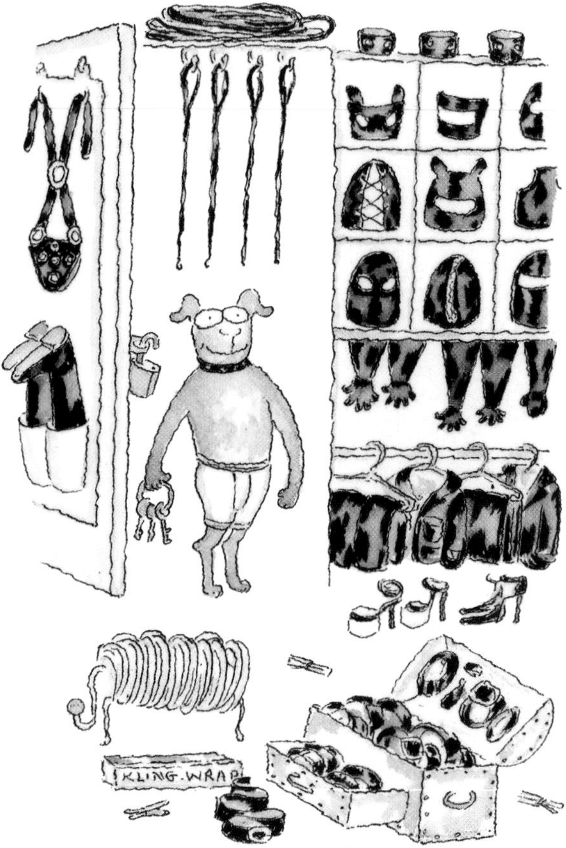
KLING WRAP

Does your dog insist on
"a room of his own"?

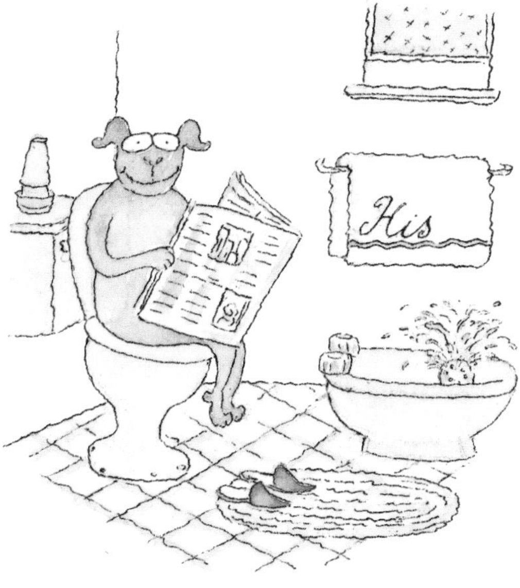
His

Does your dog run with
a faster pack than you do?

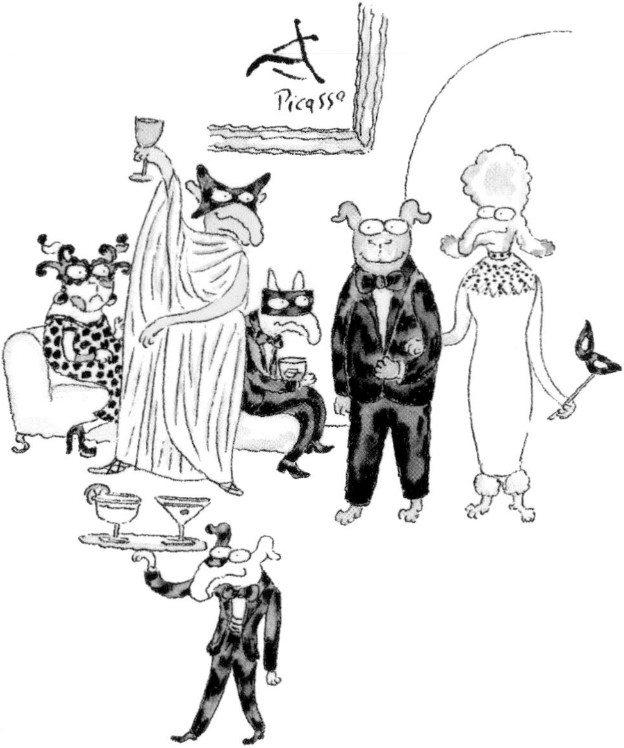
Picasso

If you answered these
questions in the affirmative,
then honey, you live with
one DIVINE dog.

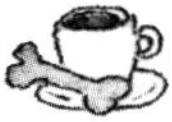